MOZART

QUARTET IN F MAJOR

T0078542

FLUTE (OBOE) AND STRINGS

KV370 (KV368b)

QUARTET IN F MAJOR

FOR

FLUTE (OBOE) AND STRINGS

OP. 8, NO. 3

STAMITZ

mmo

3308

Music Minus One

3308

Wolfgang Amadeus Mozart
Quartet in F major
for Flute (Oboe) and Strings
KV370 (KV368b)

COMPLETE VERSION TRACK	MINUS FLUTE TRACK	SECTION	PAGE
	7	Tuning Notes: A440	
1	**8**	I. *Allegro*	3
2	**9**	II. *Adagio*	6
3	**10**	III. Rondo: *Allegro*	7

Karl Stamitz
Quartet in F major
for Flute (Oboe) and Strings
op. 8, no. 3

COMPLETE VERSION TRACK	MINUS FLUTE TRACK	SECTION	PAGE
4	**11**	I. *Allegro*	11
5	**12**	II. *Andante*	13
6	**13**	III. *Presto*	14

Quartet in F major

KV370 (KV368b)

FLUTE (OBOE)

Wolfgang Amadeus Mozart
(1756-1791)

4

II.

III. Rondo

8

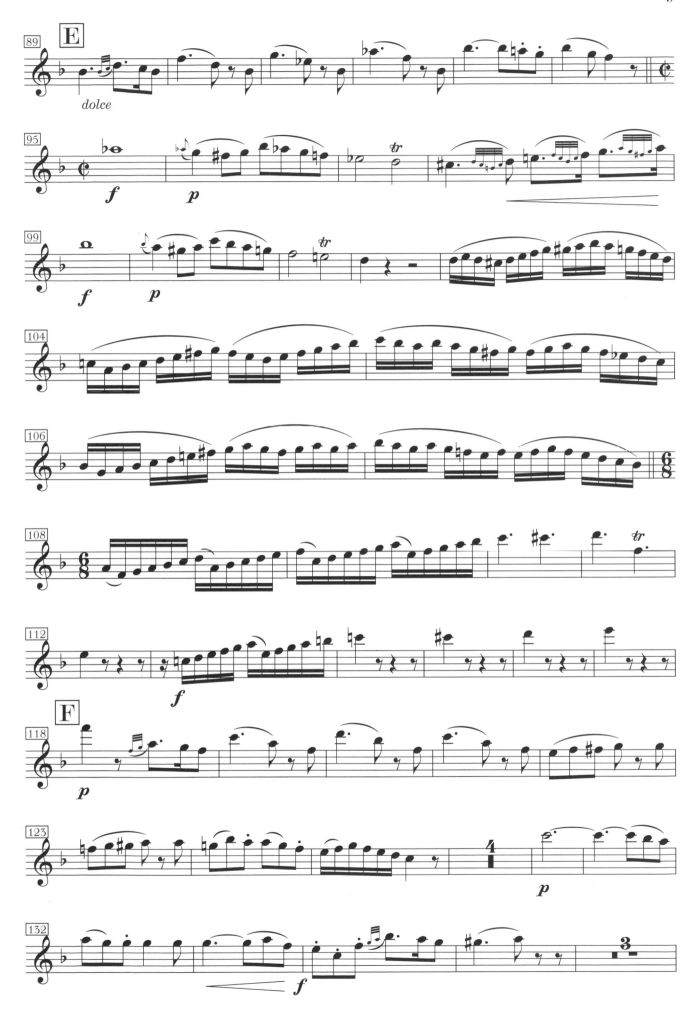

Quartet in F major
OP. 8, NO. 3

FLUTE (OBOE)

Karl Stamitz
(1745-1801)

5 12 *4 taps (1 measure) precede music*

Andante

14

6 13 *2 taps (1 measure) precede music.*

Presto

15

Engraving: Wieslaw Novak

MMO 3308

SUGGESTIONS FOR USING THIS MMO EDITION

WE HAVE TRIED to create a product that will provide you an easy way to learn and perform an ensemble piece with a full accompaniment in the comfort of your own home. Because it involves a fixed performance, there is an inherent lack of flexibility in tempo. The following MMO features and techniques will reduce these inflexibilities and help you maximize the effectiveness of the MMO practice and performance system:

Where the soloist begins a movement *solo*, we have provided an introductory measure with subtle taps inserted at the actual tempo before the soloist's entrance.

Chapter stops on your CD are conveniently located throughout the piece at the beginnings of each movement, and are cross-referenced in the score. This should help you quickly find a desired place in the music as you learn the piece.

We have observed generally accepted tempi, but some may wish to perform at a different tempo, or to slow down or speed up the accompaniment for practice purposes. You can purchase from MMO (or from other audio and electronics dealers) a specialized CD player which allows variable speed while maintaining proper pitch. This is an indispensable tool for the serious musician and you may wish to look into purchasing this useful piece of equipment for full enjoyment of all your MMO editions.

We want to provide you with the most useful practice and performance accompaniments possible. If you have any suggestions for improving the MMO system, please feel free to contact us. You can reach us by e-mail at mmogroup@musicminusone.com.

MUSIC MINUS ONE
50 Executive Boulevard
Elmsford, New York 10523-1325
800-669-7464 (U.S.)/914-592-1188 (International)
www.musicminusone.com
e-mail: mmogroup@musicminusone.com

MMO 3308

Printed in Canada